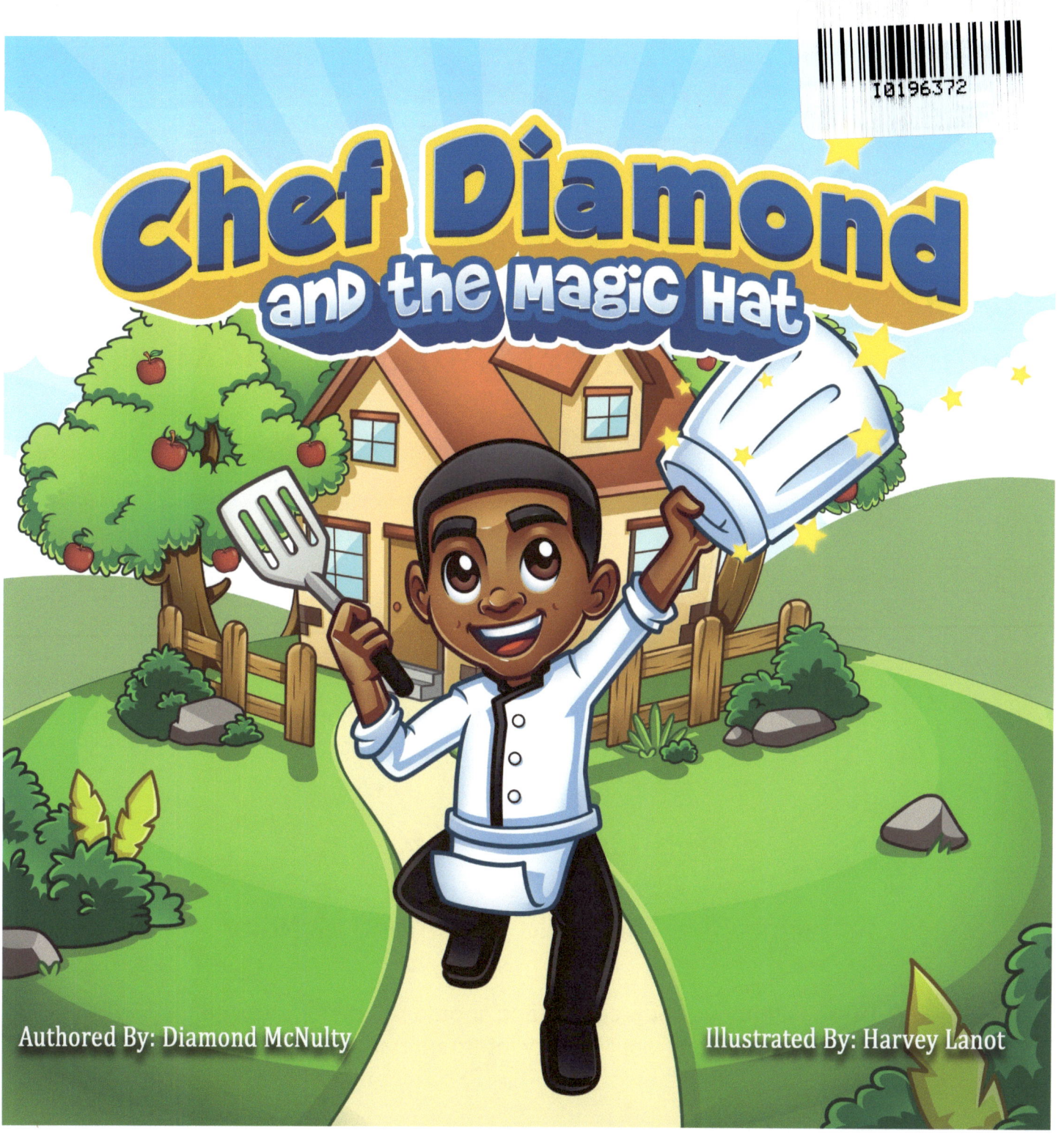

Dedicated to my grandma "Aunt Shirley" Mitchell

Copyright © 2018 McNulty International LLC
All Rights Reserved.

ISBN-13: 978-1945318054
ISBN-10: 1945318054
"Taking Over The World" - Diamond McNulty

Pages within this book cannot and should not be reproduced
without written permission from McNulty International LLC. All Rights Reserved

Chef Diamond and The Magic Hat

Created By: Diamond McNulty

Once upon a time, there lived a little boy named Diamond.

He was named Diamond because when he was born he had a bright twinkle in his eyes.

Diamond was raised in a neighborhood where the people were poor and didn't have much to call their own.

Although he lived in a small apartment and didn't have many friends to play with, Diamond was a very happy child with a really big smile on his face.

Diamond had a big dream to become a Chef when he grew up!

He told his mom, dad, his sister Lisa and everybody else he met, that he wanted to be a Chef.

Diamond was very attached to his grandmother and he loved to visit her house because he would get to watch her cook.

So on weekends, his mom would drop him off at his grandmother's house.

"Hey Diamond, how wonderful to see you!" his grandmother would greet him with a kiss on his chubby cheeks.

One weekend, his grandmother asked, "Diamond, what would you like to be when you grow up?"

Diamond replied with a twinkle in his eyes, "Grandma, I want to be a Chef!!!"

"Hmmm…now let me see if I can help you," his grandmother said thoughtfully.

Then she went to her closet and began throwing out items on to the ground… there were clothes, bags, shoes, and…

Guess what she pulled out next?

A Chef Hat!

Grandmother said to Diamond, "This is not an ordinary hat; this is a very special hat.
This is a Magical Chef Hat!"

Then grandmother placed the Magical Chef Hat on Diamond's head!

Diamond was excited and happy.

Then grandmother said, "You can become anything you want to be in life if you believe in yourself!"

"From now onwards I shall call you Chef Diamond!" Grandmother exclaimed.

His grandmother's words were very encouraging. Chef Diamond knew his grandmother had great wisdom.

He hugged his grandmother and said, "I believe I can do anything I set my mind on…
I'm going to take over the world!"

And so Chef Diamond watched as his grandmother cooked her famous Gumbo.

She was very graceful and a pleasure to watch. He realized that cooking could be so much fun!

After enjoying a delicious dinner, Chef Diamond's mother came to pick him up from his grandmother's house.

On his ride home, Chef Diamond was excited and he began telling his mother all of his dreams in life.

He said, "Mom I'm going to be a great Chef! I'm going to have a big house and I'm going to buy you a big house as well!"

His mother smiled with love.

As they arrived back to their apartment building. Chef Diamond looked around at his neighborhood – and that's when reality struck.

There were empty cans scattered all over the ground and there were people sleeping outside in the open; they were homeless people.

Chef Diamond's big dream of becoming a great Chef didn't match the reality that he lived in a neighborhood that had little to boast about.

But Chef Diamond wasn't ready to give up on his big dream, oh, no.

He said with eager determination, "I will help everyone… I will take over the world!"

That evening, after brushing his teeth, and saying his prayers Chef Diamond placed his Magical Chef Hat on his nightstand before bed.

The next morning Chef Diamond jumped up from bed; early before his mother, and ran into her room yelling, "Mom, mom wake up!
When I get older I am going to make the world a better place! Can I help you cook breakfast this morning?"

His mother smiled as she replied, "Yes son, you will make the world a better place, and I believe in you. Go grab your Magic Chef Hat and you can help me cook breakfast this morning."

Together Chef Diamond and his mom made whole wheat pancakes, eggs, cooked oatmeal and fresh orange juice.

Once breakfast was ready, Chef Diamond went to wake up his older sister Lisa.
He would always call her, "Lisa, Bisa.

Lisa Bisa, wake up it's time for breakfast."

During breakfast Lisa said, "Hey Chef, you did a great job! The food looks and tastes delicious,"

Mom chimed in, "Yes he did, Great job Chef! Keep up the great work and one day you will become a Master Chef.

Now let's clean up the kitchen."

www.ingramcontent.com/pod-product-compliance
Lightning Source LLC
Chambersburg PA
CBHW042124040426
42450CB00002B/59